Bouvier des Flanders Dogs as Pets

A Pet Care Guide for Bouvier des Flanders

Bouvier des Flanders General Info, Purchasing, Care, Cost, Keeping, Health, Supplies, Food, Breeding and More Included!

By Lolly Brown

Copyrights and Trademarks

Disclaimer and Legal Notice

Foreword

One of the hardest working dogs around, the Bouvier de Flanders is a medium-to-large sized dog with a heavy, wiry coat which comes in a variety of colors. It originates from Belgium and believed to be the descendants of Scottish deerhounds and Irish wolfhounds crossed bred and mated with working dogs in and around farms across Europe. Others say working dogs were bred out to the Mastiff, the Sheepdog and certain spaniels. No matter how many varieties of breed were used one thing was sure, they were all bouviers who had the strong working class traits of these dogs.

It is called to be one of the hardest working dogs in the region of Europe because of the great contributions it has given to the many facets of society. From flanking the sides of brave soldiers, acting as messenger between camps during war time, to aiding in security and protection, to guardian dogs to families, the Bouvier de Flanders has taken many roles and so much more!

Table of Contents

Chapter One: The Bouvier de Flanders:

A History in Brief

Originating from shores of Belgium and the farms along its countryside, the bouvier de flanders was recognized and largely bred for its hard working abilities and innate herding skills. A stocky, solid-built, medium sized dog with dense, a wiry coat, the bouvier de flanders has been utilized to help farmers, shepherds and livestock growers to round up herds and keep order.

It was also a well utilized dog during the 1st World War. Bravely going to and from camps, it would deliver vital messages, transmit communications and serve as an alert dog for the soldiers it accompanied. It had almost gone extinct a couple of times during times of war and unrest. Bouvier des flandres because of their strong bones and powerful physique were often used as ambulance dogs who helped wounded and injured soldiers. They did the dangerous job of detecting mines making a clear path for oncoming soldiers. Many of them lost due to landmines, gunshots and the many perils of being in the thick of the battle.

However with the aid of lovers of this canine sort, the bouvier de flanders has managed to rally on and continues to be enjoyed today by many. A pretty controversial dog in its own right, the Bouvier de Flanders is a canine that is still in the spotlight. It almost went into extinction back during the Second World War. As a result of the observations of the bouvier being a fiercely hardworking, the ruthless leader, Hitler, asked to meet with one. And the results that followed became the contention and beginning of a controversy that still resonates up to this day.

The canine that was said to have met with Hitler was said to have taken one whiff of the leader and bit him on the family jewels. Another report says that Hitler offered the dog his hand and was immediately bitten by the dog. From then on, all bouvier de flanders, it is said, became an "enemy of the state" and it was whispered that Hitler had set an all-out assault on the wiry - coated bouvier de flanders. Many say that this is a myth or a half-truth. Some war history buffs say that it was in fact the hand of Hitler which the dog nipped and after that, the bouvier de flanders landed on Hitler's extinction list.

It was the good doctor Dr. Adolphe Reul, from the Veterinary School of Brussels who pointed out the many exemplary qualities of the bouvier de flanders which called the attention of dog breeders from all over. Back then, the bouvier des flancers stood at around 26 inches from its shoulders, it had a heavy-set, cylindrical physique. It looked rough around the edges with wild-growth of curly fur in the colours of fawn, black or gray.

The Earlier Life of the Bouvier

The dog was first spotted on the northern French countryside, in Northwest Flanders. The bouvier de flanders was observed to be a strong, boisterous, well-utilized beast with many roles around the farm. The hardworking, active canine was used to herd cattle and give protection as it guarded farm as well as livestock.

The farmer and owners of the canine required help going about the task of churning butter, and the canine was a big part in the completion of this task. They were also used to mill, haul carts to bring produce and products to sell to the market. The Bouvier de Flanders was known by many different names, and many of these names are still used to this day. Some called it the Vuilbaard, which means dirty beard. There were those who called it the Koehond, loosely translated as cow dog and the Toucheur de Boeuf or the "cattle driver."

It was butchers, cattle keepers and merchants, as well as farmers who were the first breeders of the bouvier de flanders. Their interest laid on the great working qualities of the canine and not so much in producing a pedigreed breed. The only intent was to develop the breed in order to have the animals be "farm hands" and apt co-workers. There was a lot of experimenting that went on and so there are accounts of bouvier de flanders being of varied sizes, colour and weight during the early days of it being bred.

All the regions around Belgium and France had their own preferred sort of bouvier which all varied in shape, size and colour. The variation of the bouvier abounded for years even after the breed standard was written up in 1912. But the one thing that held them all together and be classified as bouviers was their shared traits and characteristics of being fierce leaders and hardworking canines.

A Soldier of War and Beyond

It was in WW1 when all sturdy working canines were sent off to do military service, and it was then again, the bouvier proved it versatility and value. Aside from delivering communication from one camp to the next, the robust canine would haul ammunition, and go in search of wounded soldiers in the battle field who needed aid. These all being very dangerous jobs which put a toll on the breed during time of war.

One bouvier survivor of war called Nic de Sottegem was rescued by a Belgian army vet. When the war ended judges of dog shows were fascinated as they examined the excellent structural quality of the brave and daring canine and was said to be highly approved. It was the offspring of Nic de Sottegem who were used to develop a new basis of a more uniform standard of Bouviers. The aim of the breeders shifted to focusing on the replication of the good points of Nic de Sottegem to replicate, populate and fine-tune the breed.

The rebuilding process to establish the bouvier began in the 1920s and coincided with the period of when the canine was able to reach the shores of the United States. It was later in 1932 when the bouvier was given recognition by the American Kennel Club. Not as a working dog but a show dog.

Let's take a look at the other traits of the bouvier de flanders in the following sections of this book and discover its many wonderful traits. Learn what you need to do in order to help draw out the good in the canine and how you can help curb misbehavior by channeling their energies through proper training and interaction with others.

Chapter Two: A Focus on The Modern Day Bouvier de Flanders

Bred to be sturdy, working dogs at the onset of the sort, the bouvier de flanders now finds its way into the hearts of many because of the strong traits it has. Considered to be a loyal and fierce protector of the stock and family it knows, it also continues to flank law and military personnel. Bouviers are by nature a very protective sort of canine and this will become truly apparent without the proper socialization and training. It is highly advised and strongly recommended for anyone who wants to take in and raise one of these boisterous pups to enroll it in a puppy kindergarten which uses positive reinforcement during training.

The young bouvier de flanders will need a strong structure of training and schooling in order to be able to curb and avoid seeming disobedience and misbehavior.

Taking it out for frequent trips outdoors where it can come across the world, meeting other dogs as well as humans, where they can explore and investigate, hear noises and smell new scents, is an ideal way of initiating and founding its socialization. These are experiences which will teach these highly intelligent dogs of appropriately honing their protective instinct and nature.

These are smart dogs not to be under estimated; they will take over the household and you if you do not take early measures of presenting yourself as alpha of the pack. Establish yourself as the boss of the household while you can carry the little pup. Little bouviers can be loud and opinionated that is not afraid of rough play and will get into it if opportunity presents itself. As much as bouviers love and go well with children it is not recommended to leave a very small child with a bouvier without responsible adult supervision.

A young adult bouvier de flanders is a compact and powerful canine with lean, muscular and tough looking physique. It is sure-footed and observed to be precise in its gait. It is known to be fearless and protective. A hardworking and efficient farm hand, it is agile, bold and spirited yet can be utterly well-behaved and serene as well. This beautiful enigma of a dog with its many wonderful traits makes for a great companion and family addition because it is one of the most loyal to its kindred.

The Attractive Looking Bouvier

The tremendous body strength of the bouvier de flanders displays itself in its compact, muscular and well-proportioned physique. Its sure footedness and display of confidence is a picture of a dog to reckon with when faced down by what it would perceive as a threat to itself or its humans. A rough and tough machine, the bouvier looks every bit the confident working dog it is. Bred to be versatile working farm canines, the bouvier de flanders can do the job as a cattle herder, a security canine or a draft dog.

The mustachioed and bearded canine has a sturdy head that is bold and striking. Its expression is attentive and alert. It has a hardy composition that is able to adjust and adapt to harsh conditions. Its coat has the appearance and touch of being wiry, harsh and dry but the undercoat of the bouvier de flanders is very fine in texture.

The watchful and ever attentive Bouvier is a very active canine and is described to be a self-assured dog in breed standards. This canine sort is well-noted to show readiness for learning and a propensity for carrying out its purpose. They are innately curious about all things and everyone around them, which makes them excellent investigators. They are top-notch security dogs and have worked beside men of valor in many, countless missions.

The Bouviers Personality

This Muscle from Brussels possesses a pleasing personality who likes to live an active lifestyle and would suit anyone who chooses to do the same. They are a calm, gentle sort who does well and can behave indoors with the proper training and early schooling. Devoted and loyal to their humans, the bouvier de flanders is a protective canine who will step between peril and their human without skipping a beat.

They can be a domineering canine if not set in its place. A naturally independent canine, you will need to remind it who is master of the household or be the one lead around with an invisible leash. It has a courageous nature and a steady personality. They are an obedient bunch but will need to get into proper socialization early in order to develop those instincts of being able to tell who is friend and foe. They have a tendency to bark at people they don't know as well as dogs they may meet. It is an obedient dog but may show aggression toward strangers.

The bouvier de flanders is certainly a breed who is made for the outdoors and will thrive best not only in the confines of your four walls. This canine is meant to be able to live indoors and needs a lot of outside time as well. Bred to work, the bouvier needs constant if not a lot of exercise. It is the perfect companion canine for those long treks, hikes, walks and jogs. Keeping it on a strict exercise regimen is highly advisable in order to allow it to thrive at its optimum level of mental and physical prowess.

As much as the bouvier de flander is a versatile dog who has gained great popularity as a show dog. In spite of it being a crowd and judge pleaser at dog shows, the true to form bouvier is still a favourite animal-helper on farms, doing what they do best - herding.

Chapter Three: The Versatile Bouvier

Keep in mind that the bouvier de flanders wears many hats. Apart from being actors and landing acting parts in TV and movies the reliably trustworthy bouvier is dauntless when called on to perform a task. It will be difficult to distract a bouvier by anything that may try to draw away its attention always ensuring professionalism at work. Known to be one of the most intelligent and highly trainable beasts, the bouvier de flanders is a breed of great skills and abilities. It is one of the most professional working dog breeds as evidenced by the farmers who employ the bouvier. I currently ranks somewhere in the top 100 dogs chosen by dog lovers everywhere.

Let us go on a quick journey of discovery and learn about the many jobs the bouvier de flanders is called to do. You will get to know about its keen abilities which allow it to help farmers and other individuals with their everyday needs. This section will also show the one-of-a-kind traits of the bouvier de flanders which make it a favoured canines in the different areas of society.

Rough and Tough Working Dogs

Calling the land of northern France and mainly the Flemish area of Belgium home, the bouvier de flanders was bred mostly by farmers, butchers and merchants. Since it was such a robust animal that was easy to have around work, it was bred and meant to help farmers herd cow - gaining its name Toucheur de Boeuf. It was also given heavier tasks like carting produce and meat product to the market. It also had the job of managing livestock whilst securing the animals and the human folk.

The active and sturdy dog was said to have been developed through a lot of experimentation by some monks at Ter Duinen, early farmers and butchers. They are said to have come about by cross breeding imported Tibetan Mastiffs, Irish Wolfhounds, Schnauzers, Brabanters, Beaucerons and/or Griffons with farm dogs of the locality.

Although this is said to be mostly heresay and there is not enough concrete evidence to support this. What is known to be sure is that from as far back as man toiled the lands they inhabited, strong, tough cattle-dogs has worked and lived in the region of Flanders and on the plains of northern France. The type of dogs that went into the gene pool, however, is still widely contested by many dog experts. What we know to be factual is that the first two Bouviers appeared in 1910 at the international dog show in Brussels. The intelligent and strongly-built canine quickly caught the eye of the Societe Royale Saint-Hubert.

With the assistance of a Frenchman, M. Fontaine, the vice-president of the Club, Saint-Hubert du Nord in 1912, a standard for the breed was adopted later that year; breeders of the bouvier de flanders came together in August of that year to create the bouvier de flanders Standard of Perfection, making it the first and official standard given recognition by the by the Societe Royale Saint-Hubert. It was when the clamour for the breed flourished.

The Keen Senses and Sensibilities of the Bouvier de Flanders

The bouvier de flanders has been, and up to this day, continues to be a breed choice to utilize as a working dog at countryside farms. The canines were apparently utilitarian. The first bouviers were quite versatile, hauling carts for butchers. They drove and guarded cattle herds for merchants. It easily found a role to play on the family farm, making good any work necessary, from operating grist mills to securing and defending the farm property from intruders.

They are especially applauded for their courageous contributions to police work and military operations. Its fortitude is unshakable and best around dangerously trying jobs like apprehending a criminal, search and rescue missions as well as detecting illegal and smuggled drugs. In addition, many bouviers have served as military canines ever since they were found to be such effective scout partners. They are trained to secure and patrol high-risk areas as they are utilized to give warning to soldiers for booby traps, or other hazards which may spell mortal danger to their troops. A good lot of these dogs were taken in by foreign servicemen who became impressed by the intelligence loyalty and obedience of the bouvier.

The Modern Day Jobs of the Bouvier

Today as much as many of them still do all sorts of jobs on farms and work alongside the law and military personnel, bouviers are known to be wonderful companion pets. They are also some of the best protection enforcers around and are great for active, single people and small families. Needless to say they have found a niche in the world completing the lives of those who need or require their company. They make perfect therapy dogs and excellent guide dogs.

Chapter Four: Health of the Bouvier de Flanders

Taking in a bouvier is not advisable for a new dog owner but if you are the brave sort bent on sharing your life with one then you need to understand that this strong, fit dog can also become vulnerable to illnesses. Knowing what to expect and is expected from you in terms of keeping your bouvier healthy. The care for its health is a responsibility that falls on your shoulders. You should also inform those who will be sharing care of the bouvier with you what it takes to maintain the health and wellness of your loyal companion.

Having to work the dangerous job of herding cattle they are often prone to injury when they work. They run the risk and often get hurt, getting trodden on and kicked by cows. The Bouvier des Flandres is a dog accustomed to harsh weather conditions and is very hardy canines who hardly ever fall ill. In a nutshell, these dogs were bred to keep on trucking despite the licking. Because of their high threshold for pain they usually will not be able to show signs or tell you WHEN or WHERE they hurt - making it harder for vets to treat them. Vets need only to manipulate body parts and limbs to identify injury or illness in other dogs, but not so much for our trusty bouvier.

Since they do have such a high threshold for pain it is absolutely imperative that the bouvier get regular checkups in order to rule out any illness or injuries to the dog. A few bouviers are vulnerable to eye problems, like cataracts, as well as elbow and hip dysplasia. An apartment dweller it can be, since they are a relatively subdued bunch and don't make much of a fuss when indoors. However, they will need a regular amount of exercise because they can get pretty stagnant when kept inside for too long. Besides, the Bouvier des Flandres is a dog meant to be outdoors.

It is an energetic dog - a vast yard where they may romp and play, would be the best home setting for them. No matter whether you live in an apartment or a house with a yard, the thing you want to remember is that the bouvier will need regular exercise, so if you are they sporty, outdoorsy type, bring your bouvier along for treks, runs or bike rides! Your bouvier will be happy to run right beside you.

Health Issues of The Bouvier de Flanders

Knowing about the health concerns and possible conditions which may affect your bouvier des flandres is something you must know, understand and be able to identify. Being aware of these conditions not only empower you to be selective when choosing breeders to deal with - understanding these ailments and symptoms of such gives you a better advantage of avoiding what needs to be avoided.

The most typical health related ailments which plague the bouvier des flanders are the outcome of the improper breeding practices early in the breed's existence, although it was deemed important to preserve the breed's other traits. Make sure that you are one who will champion the advocacy of keeping the bouvier breed healthy

Hip and Elbow Dysplasia

One of the more common medical conditions of the very active and utterly hardworking bouvier is hip dysplasia. This condition could eventually lead to the canine having to endure arthritic pain later in its life if not given the proper treatments. A proper diet rich in all the needs of a bouvier would also help it along in the management of hip dysplasia.

Hip dysplasia can be recognized as the dog having difficulty in getting up, a reluctance to play, hardship climbing up a flight of steps, hopping and trotting are some of the more obvious symptoms of this. Elbow dysplasia exhibits as lameness in the forelimbs of the dog a diminished ability to flex, extend and hyperextend the front legs. A bouvier suffering from this may not put any weight at all on its front legs.

Subaortic Stenosis

Subaortic stenosis is a problem that affects dogs and can usually be detected early in the life of a afflicted bouvier. Most commonly occurring in large-breed dogs, subaortic stenosis appears to autosomal recessive in these dogs; the first signs of it may be present at birth (moderate or severe cases) or the usually milder cases may become apparent in the first year. It is around the 12 month age of the bouvier when the Orthopedic Foundation for Animals provides a certification clearing the bouvier of subaortic stenosis

Glaucoma

This is a condition that affects the sight of the dog, wherein pressure is put upon the eye, resulting in inadequate drainage of fluids from the eyes. Should the condition becomes chronic or persist without treatment; it will cause permanent damage to the optic nerve, resulting in blindness. Glaucoma was noted to be more common in Bouviers from the Netherlands noting the commonality of feature affecting the left eye of the dog. Dogs with poor drainage angles are the ones most susceptible to the condition which is thought to be polygenic.

Symptoms are not to be ignored and these come forth as behavioural changes in the canine. Eyes are glassy during early stages, excessive "weepy" eye, redness of the blood vessels in the upper whites of the eyes, cloudy appearance of the eye, sensitivity to light, wanting to sleep all the time, behaviour indicating pain, dilated pupil – or when the pupil does not respond to light, vision impairment or total loss of vision.

Hypothyroidism

When the immune system attacks the thyroid gland of the animal, destruction of the thyroid happens. It is a disease of the metabolism which results from the deficiency of two thyroid gland hormones called thyroxine (T4) and triiodothyronine (T3). Primary Hypothyroidism results from the atrophy of the thyroid gland. Secondary hypothyroidism is a lack of TSH or thyroid stimulating hormone - this could be congenital or acquired. In the case of adult dogs it is usually apparent with a tumor of the pituitary gland.

Symptoms include hair loss, weight gain, and rough skin. The affected dog can develop facial folds, accompanied by reduced mental alertness, gives it a sad, tragic look. The dog may seem cold to the touch, its rectal temp may read lower than usual. Bowel functions change in consistency and regularity from dry feces to occasional diarrhea. Other endocrine and hormonal diseases reportedly developed or manifested by bouviers is Cushing's disease as well as Addison's disease.

Cancer

This is the number one disease that kills dogs each year. Cancer appears when cells subdivide and grow when not needed, turning them into tumors. Tumors are able to travel through the blood and find its way to other parts of the body. A spreading cancer is called metastasis. Cancer is diagnosed through a battery of tests including the collection and study of the sample tissue and checked by a pathologist. Early detection is the key to survival. Behavioral changes can become apparent from a once healthy bouvier. An affected one could show loss of appetite, persistent coughing and wheezing, abnormal swelling in parts of the body, sores that do not heal. The affected dog may find it difficult to chew and/or swallow, may have difficulty breathing, and moving bowel/passing urine.

Prevent Health Problems

There are some vaccinations that, if given too frequently, could weaken the immune system of your bouvier and this could make it vulnerable to illness. The wrong vaccines could make the dog very ill as well. Not only is it imperative for you to find out more about the pros and cons of vaccinating your dog, you should also seek out the most up-to-date vet whose concern is to help you raise a healthy dog. Many pet products out in the market can actually be toxic to our furry friends. Learn to read and decipher manufacturer labels, this will help you avoid making the wrong decisions about things you get for your canine's usage.

Raising a healthy bouvier would mean that you would have to do some investigative work on the parental history of the canine. Have both, bitch and stud, been tested for hip and elbow dysplasia, inherited eye-conditions and heart disease? These are some of the important questions you will need answered when you start talking to a breeder. And then, feeding your bouvier the wrong sorts of food could and can cause your big dog from Flanders to develop chronic health issues, such as oily or dry skin and hair, itching, ear infections, gas, runny or loose stools, infections and a host of other illnesses and diseases.

There are chew toys which can cause a host of uncomfortable conditions to dogs. The wrong ones can cause vomiting or diarrhea. Others can cause choking. Improper chew toys can cause intestinal blockage to the dog as well.

Chapter Five: Maintenance of Bouvier des Flander Breed

The bouvier de flanders is a bold, yet well-mannered canine who fears very little. It is difficult to distract the calm and self-possessed bouvier. Being a thoughtful dog as well as one with excellent instincts, the bouvier de flanders will only react when he deems the company unsavory. A well trained bouvier responds only with the most precise actions necessary for the moment. It relies on its sound judgment, and is able to size up situations accordingly. Not the aggressive one unless it senses danger, it prefers to surprise unwanted with collected scrutiny of the situation.

Introduce early training to the canine. It is imperative that the bouvier learns to respect its human's authority. The growing bouvier can be quite rowdy during adolescence and can try to push the limits. It can get pretty excited during playtime so you should not leave them alone with small children. While the bouvier is an excellent companion it is not free of its rough edges. Find out more about how to socialize, care for and maintain the bouvier de flanders in the next section.

To Leash or Not to Leash? - When to Keep the Leash Off

The bouvier des flanders is one of the most loyal dogs around and is very protective toward its human wards. However, do not make the mistake of tethering your bouvier des flanders to a post for too long in your yard. This type of restraint will lead to certain frustration of your bouvier and unwelcome aggression. Make sure that you are with your bouvier des flanders when it is outside and do not allow your bouvier to roam free on its own in the neighborhood or you might have to face neighbor complaints. This will also help avoid canines in the area from warring with other dogs.

Your new and young bouvier des flanders will be most happy living indoors with you and the rest of the family members. But make sure you allow it frequent access to a big space within a fenced in yard so that it can spend some of its energy positively. Raising your bouvier indoors for part of the time will require you to make room for it inside your home. Make sure to delegate spaces around the house for the bouvier to retreat to after a tiring day of work and play. Situate a crate in a social area of the home like a hallway or beneath an indoor planter. Prepare for it a sleeping area where it can lay down at the end of the day.

Allot a space in the kitchen and where your bouvier can have its meals in peace. Pay mind to choose slow-feeding dishes to discourage your dog from scarfing down its food too fast.

Training and Socialization

No one is more loyal than bouviers to their human family. They deeply love and is happiest when it is around its humans. It is the magnet of the family gently nudging each one back when separated. It can be a pretty difficult adolescent pup to live with; hence, early schooling is highly advised. The bouvier des flandres, more than anything, needs mind stimulation the most. It needs to be able to channel all the smarts it possesses in positive areas or they can be a great handful.

A good balance of kindness and firmness is important to employ during the early training period of the young bouvier because it can be quite a handful. It has a sharp memory so do not try repetitive training sessions because it will bore easily. The bouvier only needs to give thought to a situation before reacting. There is no better time to start training school than when it is young. About 8 weeks old is a good time to get the puppy in puppy manners school. This is when they are sponges and are at the prime for learning. A smart bouvier will need to be engaged mentally frequently and if not given this opportunity to learn to deduce for itself, it could channel all that energy negatively.

Highly intelligent with great instincts to boot, the bouvier is an outstanding guard dog who would loyally stand by your side and be the first in line should it deem a situation a threat. Should he learn and understand to respect your authority the bouvier de flanders will obey you. Given the quick study it is, all you need is to allow it a second to think about what you call for it to do. Enhance its skills and abilities and allow the bouvier to learn how to hone these on its own as it grows. You, your family and your bouvier will be happier because of it.

If the needs and requirements of the bouvier are supplied for and provided, the bouvier can be a well-mannered dog. Give it a daily chore to do around the home in order for it to feel useful family member. Treat it like the intelligent being it is and it will reward you with its loyalty. A bouvier is meant to work, it is meant to work with its mind. Giving it chores and stuff to do around the house allows the bouvier to become engaged in your daily routines and gives it the opportunity to do what it is meant to do.

Exercise and Play

Make sure that as it grows it is given the proper mind and body stimulation to encourage it to develop its skills and abilities to its finest. Allow it time outside to exercise for it to keep its physique in top condition. A bouvier will gladly run alongside you when you cycle, run or take a brisk walk. It is the perfect companion for outdoorsy people who lead an active lifestyle. As it grows up allow it time outside in a controlled environment where it can learn to explore the world outside of your four walls but still be within bounds of your stead's safety. If you are going to raise one in a home with you yard you might want to start making provisions for a fence that is at least 5 feet high. Avoid electronic collars on your super smart pet, it is almost impervious to these devices.

The bouvier was developed to be a working dog therefore it is, by nature, robust and active. It is agile and not at all clumsy in its footing. It is dexterous as it is practiced.

Having many skills and an outstanding instinct, the bouvier is also an upstanding guide dog to take on trails and long treks on foot. If you are away from home for extended periods of time, then you will want to rethink the idea of taking in a bouvier. Being the active and intelligent dog it is, you will need to spend a good deal of time with the dog in order for it to be engaged in various activities. Remember to give it a job or two around the house and to balance that with optimum food and maintenance.

A bouvier can get easily bored. Leaving it alone for lengths at a time can make it anxious and could likely express their dismay and disapproval in what we would call "mischievous, but is in fact just them letting off steam. Bored dogs can start gnawing on shoes or furniture. They may display their displeasure of being left alone by digging up planters and/or flower beds. And they could frazzle your nerves with loud, continuous barking that won't win you or your dog Neighbor of the Year Award.

Keep your bouvier busy and give it responsibilities around the house. Whether at work, at play or when teaching it something new, keep in mind that the physical and intellectual stimulation is important in order for a bouvier to stay efficient. Being a smart and active dog, an experienced dog owner would know that the active bouvier will need to be engaged to help it thrive and maintain its positive traits.

A good, stretch outside for a brisk run, a walk, a game of catch or Frisbee will all do the trick of keeping your bouvier active. Make sure that you seek out a recently successful trainer to work with you and your bouvier. Make sure that you make time and are a part of its training period since it will be you from whom the bouvier will take commands. Mental stimulation through early canine training will be an utmost requirement for its discipline and overall well-being.

Grooming

Because of its elaborate, whorl coat, the bouviers grooming is an absolute necessity to carry out weekly with at least a few visits a year to a professional groomer to remove extra hair from between its paw pads. With regular grooming the shedding of the bouvier will be kept in check. Taking care of the grooming requirements of the bouvier is a little trickier than grooming the coat of other canines. Because of the fur density, the whorl outer coat and the finer underlying one, a little preparation is needed before you bathe the active, explorer, our bouvier. The time when you give your bouvier a good brushing will also be an opportune time to check its skin, stomach and limbs. Remember that the overall health of any pet, whatever breed they are will be reflected in its coat and skin. A smooth fur, free of matting and tangles, is an indication of proper maintenance and nutrition. A skin free of bald patches, rashes and nicks is a skin to be envied.

Prior to giving it bath, which you can do depending on how active your dog is, you will need to use a blower to dry out wet areas and make an effort to remove as much debris from its fur as best you can. Next step is to employ a sturdy brush and run it on the coat of the bouvier, careful not to miss any matting and tangling.

Hand stripping the coat of a bouvier has been practiced for many years and doing so allows the coat to maintain its harsh texture whilst keeping it weather resistant. You may need to use a pair of shears or a blender to even out the look but never cut too close or style too much, since the standard look of the bouvier calls for it to be tousled, and wiry in appearance. Make sure that you get the services of a proper groomer and sit in during the sessions in order to learn how to strip our bouviers coat correctly before doing it on your own. Make sure that you teach this skill to another responsible member or older child of your family. Involve them in the raising of your young bouvier so that they too may reap the rewards of living with a bouvier.

Oral Care

The halitosis emitted from the mouth of a bouvier can be quite objectionable and offensive but you will still need to investigate from where this stems. It could be due to improper diet, it can also be bad smelly bacteria brought about by the buildup of plaque. It could also be brought about by gum disease, however there could be other underlying health issues causing the halitosis. If the breath of your bouvier smells like urine or ammonia, the dog could be suffering from a kidney disease. It could be suffering from liver or intestinal disease. A fruity scent from the mouth could signal diabetes. Make sure that you always remember to mention the oral care of your bouvier to your vet and pay mind to its smell of its mouth, no matter how offensive.

You should take your bouvier des flanders to get good mouth cleaning from a professional groomer and maintain its oral care by brushing its teeth at least twice a week. Use a vet approved toothpaste along with a swatch of nylon stockings or medical gauze; you may also use a toothbrush for this task.

Chapter Six: Nourishment and Sustenance

Much like us humans, canines are unique beasts with distinct needs and quirks which vary and differ from one dog to the other. They will not all need the same portion or frequency of feeding as it grows up. How much it eats will be based largely on the age, size, build, metabolism, and level of activity of the bouvier.

A very active dog will certainly require more nourishment than a more subdued one. Quality of food you purchase and feed your bouvier also plays a huge factor to its wellness. As you bouvier grows pay mind about the amount of food, you set out for it.

You also want to watch the frequency of feeding. An optimum sort of dog food will most definitely go toward nourishing your canine efficiently and as a result, you won't need to put out as much of it into your dog's feeding bowl. The big bred, hardworking and muscled canine requires optimum food to be able to thrive well and for it to stay healthy. All that luxurious hair and strong muscles will need the best quality protein and fat foods for it to be able to think and do its jobs right. If you are a brave first time dog owner bent on taking in the companionship of a bouvier, you need to know that what you feed your canine will largely affect its health.

A well fed puppy and dog is able to utilize its deduction abilities well and apply them accordingly. Make sure that it is given the proper sort of food. Provide it with the correct nutritional balance and enjoy each day with your healthy bouvier.

What to Feed Your Bouvier and How Often

The best food for your bouvier de flanders is fresh, real, non-commercial, non-processed foods. Real turkey, chicken, beef, fish, lamb mixed in with at least 10% of its diet, some fruits and vegetables is the best food to feed your growing bouvier. Don't forget to mix in a little dairy in yogurt and egg forms to complete its nourishment.

Making the correct choices about the food selection you serve it will pay off in the long run. A well-nourished canine and one raised on a proper diet will reflect on their appearance, physique, temperament and abilities of the bouvier. Be sure to study up on how you can. Stay away from all the marketing hype which is basically a smoke screen meant to disguise unnecessary ingredients. Learn to decipher the meaning behind flowery label-wording and photos which portray happy, smiling pets.

A small bouvier des flandres puppy aged between 8 to 12 weeks will need to be fed at least 4 small meals per day. Feeding frequency changes and will noticeably lesson as it grows. Three meals per day will be required of the 3-6 month old bouvier. A six to twelve-month pup can be fed twice a day. When your bouvier reaches its first birthday, once a day feedings will be sufficient but then again there are some bouviers which prefer two light bowls given at intervals during the day. So make sure to observe the eating schedule of your bouvier. Be sure to network with other caregivers of bouvier des flanders. Your diligence in observation will not only allow you to get to know your bouvier better, it will also allow you to share best practices with others. Strive to improve the breed and be part of that advocacy.

Home Cooked Food

More and more canine owners demand only the finest of high grade ingredients to provide the proper sustenance of their dogs. And pet food manufacturers have heard this as they have stepped up, coming out with impressively well-balanced variations of natural pet foods. These can be quite costly in the long run, but it is an option you have.

Due to the financial dent prime quality dog foods make on the budget of owners, canine lovers have started looking more into home cooking for their pets. Not only is this a healthier choice it is also more economical. You also get to control the freshness of the food you serve your dog. Food you feed you bouvier which you made in your kitchen, saves you money in the long run and you get to also give it some variety. Homemade meals are prepared diets typically recommended by holistic practicing veterinarians. Homemade meals would usually include cooked or raw meats with a bit whole grains, a portion raw vegetables and a variety of nutritional supplements.

Try to get a recipe from a vet who has expertise in nutrition, or an experienced bouvier dog owner who has been feeding their bouvier home prepared meals. When chosen and cooked well, home prepared meals can be an extremely healthy choice for your new bouvier des flanders.

Types of Food Needed

For an all-natural dog food to be labeled all-natural, manufacturers need to follow strict guidelines. These guidelines indicate that all the ingredients used as well as parts of the ingredients used present in the food has to be naturally occurring. Should any of the components be chemically synthesized, the label must state this clearly.

You can mix canned or wet food with some water and broth. You can do the same with premium-grade dry food. High-grade dry food ensures a balanced diet to an adult bouvier but make sure to mix it up with some dairy foods in the form of cottage cheese, or a cooked egg. You may also add some fruits and veggies to its diet but make should that it only makes up 10% of its daily food allowance. Provide it plenty of fresh clean water using only clean dishes at all times.

Types of Food to Avoid

Do not, under any circumstances offer your bouvier alcoholic drinks. No caffeine based drinks either including tea, coffee, or chocolate drinks. You are not to feed it raisins, grapes, onions, garlic or chives. No unripe fruits. Do not give it poultry bones which could lodge in its throat or worse find its way into its stomach and scar its intestinal tract. Apart from the list we have compiled remember to avoid, if not, limit, the offering of human food to a bouvier. Giving it human food may cause it to have an improper diet. Giving it human food will also risk the dog of vitamin and mineral deficiencies as well as develop bone and teeth conditions which affect its overall wellness, well-being, not to mention comfort. It could also cause the dog to become choosy with what it eats that can lead to malnutrition.

Human food, spoilt food and the like is to be avoided at all costs. There are seasonings and additives which are present in human food that can pose health hazards to the bouvier. Be mindful about what you feed it as the overall health of the bouvier also rests on its diet. Remember to measure out the proper portions of food for your growing bouvier pup. Giving it too much may pave the way for obesity, another condition most canines are prone especially if not given the proper exercise. Knowing how much your dog needs to eat is important not only to your dog's health but it is also for your financial benefit. Putting out too much food can be wasteful.

Keep in mind to clear dishes of uneaten food within the hour that you feed your bouvier. If a bouvier has not finished its food, leave it there and allow it to come back to it with the hour of the feeding. Should it not eat the remainder of the food, take mental note of the portion and subtract that much next time you feed your bouvier, but make sure to clear it out soon after as exposed food spoils easily.

Fresh Water in Abundance

Water is requirement of your actively, robust and hardworking bouvier des flanders. Water not only aids in its digestion, water also helps flush the toxins out, helping in maintaining a constant body temperature. Always make it a point to keep all feeding and water dishes clean. Doing so maintains the integrity and freshness of the intake of food and water of your bouvier des flanders.

A rise of temperature when they are outdoors causes the dog to pant. Panting allows dogs to circulate needed air to cool down. An active dog is twice likely to get petered out after a good run. Both puppies and dogs can lose a considerable amount of water through exercise. If a dog is dehydrated by more than 12% it will die. Access to water allows your bouvier to maintain its correct water balance by itself. When you go out for a walk or a run, whether on a hot day or not, bring a drink for your dog as well. Not having enough fresh water available to them may lead up to your bouvier des flanders becoming dehydrated. It could also cause the dog to form a bad habit of gulping huge quantities of water. That is bad for the dog.

Remember that the long term health of your bouvier des flanders, will largely depend on the quality of food you feed it. Feeding your bouvier premium, dog food, gives it a gift of living a quality-filled life. Their coats are healthier. They incur fewer chances with bouts of allergies. They have lesser medical issues and conditions and they develop a healthier disposition and a well-rounded personality.

Chapter Seven: How to Acquire a Bouvier des Flandres

There are a few avenues you can take when in search for a bouvier des flandres. However you want to make sure that you avoid the usual pitfalls dog lovers fall into. There will be places you want to avoid, and people you want to seek out. There will be questions for you to ask and you want to ask the correct ones. A true animal lover will want to make sure that the breed they get is a breed that they intend to keep at its optimum by employing only the best care.

You will want to do research on the people you shall eventually do business with and you also want to make sure that anything and everything you discuss with them is on the up and up. A new dog owner is typically advised not to pair up with the independent bouvier. It is known that a bouvier would need the strong leadership of its human for it to thrive socially and in order for it to carry out what it is developed to do, which is to serve and protect. However, experienced bouvier owners would disagree with this because it is not so much the inexperience that will be a challenge being a new dog owner and choosing a bouvier, but it is the commitment, discipline and consistency you are willing to extend to the time with the bouvier that matters.

Should you be a new dog owner and have your heart set on a bouvier, you also need to teach who to get in touch with to ensure a better chance of raising a well-rounded bouvier. History of parents is crucial to the wellness of any pedigreed canine as much as nourishment. Discover the essential traits of good breeders to know how to rule out bad ones.

Finding a Reputable Breeder

The future health and wellness of any pedigreed animal hinges on two things; first is the history the bouviers parents as well as the method used by breeders to mate the dogs. Nutrition and quality of food comes at a very close second.

It is of utmost importance that you determine the methods of breeding dogs.Steer clear of pet stores and puppy mills. These ill-operated, ill-informed establishments propagate the raise in health issues apparent in many animals today. Do not support these places from furthering their shady operations and do not do business with them. If you do, understand that you will be setting yourself up for a mountain of medical bills, avoidable anxiety and possible heartache. The sufferings of a bouvier pup who inherits medical conditions through substandard breeding practices can be painful to go through and can definitely be avoided.

Make certain that a canine is in the pink of health, is covered with a guarantee and has certificates and receipts to back up claims. Never buy from an irresponsible breeder, a pet store or a puppy mill or your problems, as well as the poor dogs', shall run aplenty.

Ill-informed breeders show no interest in following standard breeding procedures to ensure the good health of a bouvier des flanders pup. Irresponsible breeders do not take into account the possible future sufferings of the canine as a result of their ill-breeding methods.

Rule Out Shady Breeders - Ask Relevant Questions

For you to sort out upstanding breeders from those who aren't, you need to be a keen observer and to ask the correct questions. Breeders who are only in it for the money will show no regard for the future well-being of the pup. They will not inquire about the family it will eventually be joining. It will not investigate if the home the pup is going to is a home that will care for the bouvier. They are interested in one thing only and that is you forking over the cash.

On the other hand, breeders of the upstanding kind will not only be open to answering questions you may have about their selection and mating methods but they would keep a records of the milestones along the way. In addition to this;

- They would be concerned about the family and home of which the pup will be part.
- They will determine if you are a sound and able guardian to this magnificent beast.

- Breeders of good repute will inquire of the bouviers imminent role in your family.

- They would be interested about the space you have for it.

- They determine that the humans who are taking in the bouvier pup are aware of the challenges and rewards of sharing home and life with a bouvier des flanders.

- They want to ensure that the young bouvier is going to be part of a family who will extend it respect, friendship kindness, and unconditional love.

- They will be curious to find out if you have sought the services of an efficient and certified vet.

- These breeders would be ready to offer a guarantee.

- They would gladly give information about the dam and sire.

- They would also be able to give recommendations of effectively caring for them.

- Breeders of good standing will welcome you to their facilities.

- These breeders make sure that you are part of the breeding process from onset to the day they hand over your healthy bouvier.

- Seek out breeders who screen their breeding canines to later deem the breeding lot fit and healthy to produce offspring. Determine that the mating dogs are free of genetic diseases which can be inherited by future puppy generations. Knowing the history of the both sire and bitch to make sure no congenital or inherited diseases later plague the litter of pups. Make sure that the mating pair is of sound temperament, calm and relaxed.

When Adoption is An Option

If you have deep pockets and a big heart to boot, adoption is another route you may want to take and know by doing so you will hereinafter be doubly rewarded with the benefits of taking in an adult bouvier and have saved from a bleak future. You need to know that adopting a bouvier, whether pup or full grown, will have its own set of challenges which could set you back financially, so be ready. These challenges will vary greatly from what one would expect when you purchase a pup from a breeder.

You may end up spending more money should the canine be coming from a home that neglected it, did not invest in proper early dog training. They could be lacking in medical care, and grooming maintenance. Other dogs may have been badly treated and did not have good human interaction.

You will also be set back financially if the canine has medical conditions that need vet attention. Still, you should ask questions about the bouvier's history wish to adopt. The likelihood of you getting straight up answers to not getting any is equal, but you should still ask. You may not get all the details of the dog's history, but your generous heart and willingness to take on the care of a possibly ill or ill-treated pet will be just what a rescue pet needs.

On the other hand, once in the fold of your welcoming family, your bouvier rescue dog would have been given a new lease in life and a stay from a bleak and an uncertain future.

Given your pure intentions and ready willingness to take in a rescue dog because of the highly intelligent bouvier, integration may not be as tough as you would think. Once your intelligent bouvier des flandres rescue comes to understand what you have done, it will not hold back in expressing gratitude. You will be enjoying its fierce loyalty and loving companionship for a very long time.

Chapter Eight: Sundries and Equipment Your Bouvier Des Flanders Will Need

Once your Bouvier des Flandres is out in the world, it will be a matter of time until it joins you and your family at home. It is very important that as you wait for the pup to wean from its mum, that you are getting your house and selves ready. There is going to be a number of things your bouvier will require to feel welcomed. Allow for a seamless transition into the family and get ready with the stuff it will need.

Make sure that you have balanced your checkbook and have figured out how a pet will impact your finances. You will need to make a considerable investment in food on a monthly basis and will also have to set aside some money for unforeseen or unplanned eventualities. Then there is the business of getting accessories, grooming tools, equipment, canine supplies, toys, and general sundries. These are important purchases to help integrate your young (or mature) bouvier des flanders to your family.

Here are some of the important things you need to shop for before you take home your new bouvier des flanders:

- **A bed** - your new addition will need a place to rest its head so get it a sturdy comfortable bed where it can rest when it's all tuckered out. Provide for it a dedicated area in the house that it can retreat to and recharge.

- **A dog crate** - a durable dog crate will serve both you and your canine buddy well for a long time to come. You will most likely want to bring your bouvier along for family trips so a crate will also conveniently double as your dog's home away from home during trips and vacations. Invest in a sturdy crate because this piece of equipment will prove worthy of the money you spend later on since you will have to transport your bouvier from one place to another. You definitely do not want to put your buddy in danger riding in a vehicle without any sort of protection. A dog crate also serves the purpose when the young pup is being potty trained; take your bouvier out from its crate during scheduled times of the day and lead it outdoors and your bouvier will soon understand that this is when it should "go do nature's call." Make sure that your bouvier empties its bowels at least twice during the poop-venture outdoors, so as not to create "accidents' around the house later.

- **Stainless steel, slow-feeding bowls** - discourage your canine from scarfing down food and drinking big gulps of water by utilizing these slow-feeding bowls for its meals and drink. The feeding owl is made to promote slow-eating, allowing your bouvier of enjoying each morsel of food you set out for it.

- **Grooming brush** - The bouvier des flanders coat is thick and wavy; if its coat is not given the proper attention it will be prone to tangling and horrible matting. Make a habit of brushing your bouvier's coat to promote the distribution of skin oils. Regular brushing also avoids the instance of skin conditions.

- **Toothbrush** - Your bouvier will need regular brushing to clean its teeth of plaque and food debris or you will have to bear the smell of its breath. Pick a toothbrush that will fit comfortably in the bouvier's mouth. Make sure that it is strong enough to withstand any mischievous biting.

- **Toothpaste** - You will also need pet approved toothpaste to effectively clean your dog's teeth. Ask your vet about the sort of cleaning paste to use.

- **A sander or nail trimmer** - Trimming your bouvier's nails will become a grooming routine and you may have to experiment on tools that your dog will least resist at the beginning. Some dogs hate when their guardians trim their nails, so it is important for you to watch and take notes about which tool it is agreeable. Make certain that you cut above the pink of the animals nail when using a cutter or guillotine because cutting through it will cause profuse bleeding and great discomfort to the canine. A sander can be gentler on a dog's senses, but the whirr of the machine may cause discomfort to the dog's hearing. A sander also tends to heat up with extended use.

- **A blanket** - a blanket relays familiar comfort to anyone and why shouldn't this too hold true for your bouvier? A blanket is a comforting place to snuggle into and can be placed on the bed of the canine for added insulation. It be moved to a more social area of the home and could double as a bed for short naps.

- **A leash** - You will need a leash on while the young bouvier undergoes training. This will come in handy and useful when you take it out for walks. Make sure that you invest on one that will last. You will probably use this more when your bouvier gets bigger. A full grown bouvier des flandres is powerfully strong so, a flimsy leash could snap making you chase after your bouvier.

- **Toys** - lots of toys will be crucial so that you can engage you're curious and smart new bouvier des flanders. Use toys to engage and stimulate the dog's body and mind. A bored dog can create a pretty awful mess when left on its own for too long or too frequently. The clever bouvier needs to be engaged physically and mentally or it will channel its energies on inanimate things around that house. A bored dog can dig on, chew on, scratch at, and push around things around your house just to occupy itself or get attention from you.

Do not encourage this behaviour. Toys can be used as well during your own personal downtime with your new bouvier.

- **A fence** - a collapsible fence is a temporary solution which can be utilized when pets are young. You can use one to create separation between existing pets and your new bouvier. It can be used to give the pet's ample time to scout out each other. What it does is serve as a safe barrier from your pets getting too close to each other before they are ready to share the same space.

You most definitely will find more things your bouvier des flanders will need to ensure a warm welcome and a happy union with with you and your family. Network with experienced bouvier des flanders owners and ask about what worked and didn't work for them. Remember that offered advice must be weighed and considered because no two dogs are alike or have the exact same needs. Ultimately, only you and some of your immediate family members - people it comes in contact with on a daily basis - will be the ones who will know the canine best.

Chapter Nine: Bouvier des Flander Standard for Showing

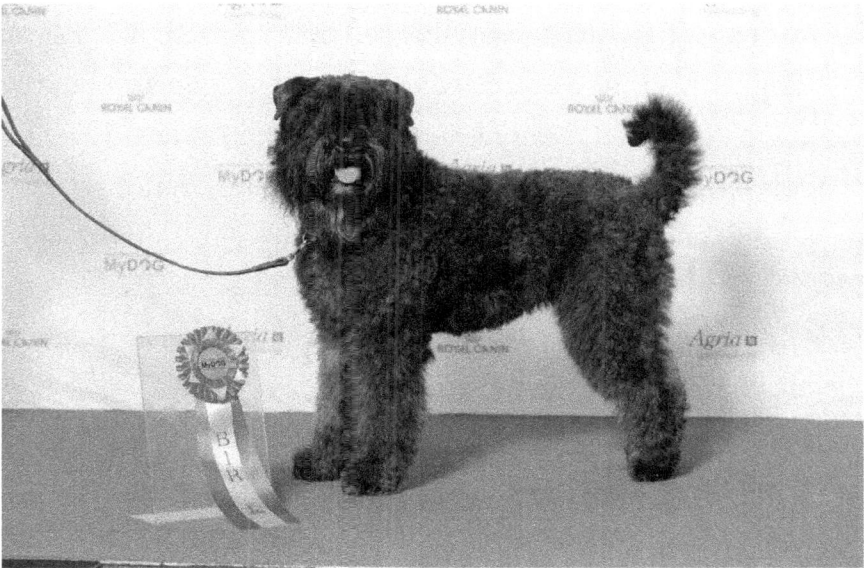

The Bouvier des Flandres is compact, large sized, rugged dog standing at an average height of 28 inches from the withers. It is a heavy boned and very powerful dog meant to toil on the fields bearing a weatherproof coat. It weighs anywhere from 70 up to 110 pounds, so, the bouvier is indeed a sizable dog with a big heart and a smart head on its shoulders. Bouviers have been bred to do almost anything in the farm from milling grist to churning butter, pulling carts, hauling merchandize, herding cows, protecting livestock as well as human dwellers of the farm.

They are big smart dogs who enjoy carrying out tasks and responds well to training. Since bouviers are such big dogs they fare better with older children. They are easily adaptable to other pets but will need some patience and time duing initial integration. Rugged and spirited, it is a serene dog that is tough and hardworking. It is agile and bold with a well-behaved manner denting its resolute, steady and fearless traits. It has a smart, brilliant gaze, denoting its intelligence, daring and vigor.

Let's take a closer look at the standards of the Bouvier des Flandres and get it ready for show!

Official Standard of the Bouvier des Flandres - American Kennel Club

General Appearance

The General Appearance of a Bouvier des Flandres is to be built powerfully. It should be compact and short-coupled. This rough-coated dog of notably rugged appearance gives the impression of great strength without any indication of being heavy or clumsy in it complete makeup.

The Bouvier des Flandres is an even-tempered dog by nature making it a great partner for farmers and acts as a cattle herder, a general farmer's helper, pulling and hauling carts, milling grist, churning butter and protecting livestock, it is an ideal farm dog. The Bouvier des Flandres is an agile, spirited and bold working dog but it is also serene, well behaved in its disposition denoting a steady, resolute and brave character. The bouviers gaze is quick, alert and brilliant - displaying his intelligence, robustness and bravery.

Its harsh double coat keeps the bouvier safe in all weather conditions, allowing it to carry out the most difficult, and arduous jobs around the farm. The bouvier has been used in many dog-jobs as an ambulance and messenger dog. Recent times find the bouvier des flanders working as a watch and guard dog for families. It is also a great companion as well as a family friend, watcher and protector.

Its physical and mental characteristics, its performance paired along with its keen senses and abilities, its intelligence and initiative allow the Bouvier des Flandres to do work as a tracking dog. The Bouvier des Flandres is also an excellent guide dog for the blind.

The following is a description that is the ideal Bouvier des Flandres. Deviations from what is mentioned here will be penalized to the degree of the departure from standards.

Size, Proportion, Substance:

Size - The height of the bouvier des flanders as measured at the withers is from 24½ to 27½ inches for dogs; bitches measure in at 23½ to 26½ inches. In either gender, the perfect measure of height is the median of the two measurement limits, i.e., 26 inches for a dog and 25 inches for a bitch. Any bitch or dog drifting from the minimum or maximum limits as said before will have to be severely penalized.

Proportion - The length of the Bouvier des Flandres beginning from the point of the shoulder up to the end of its buttocks is to be equal to the height from the floor to the utmost point of the withers. A long-bodied canine has to be gravely faulted.

Substance - The Bouvier des Flandres is powerfully built. It is powerful and strong boned, as it is well muscled, showing no signs of being heavy or being clumsy.

Head

The head of the Bouvier des Flandres, in scale, is an impressive one, highlighted by a distinct beard and a mustache. The powerful bouvier is in proportion to its body and build with an expression that is both bold and alert. Their vigilant eyes neither protrude nor are they sunken in its sockets. When viewed from the front, the shape of their eyes is oval bearing the axis on the horizontal plane. The colour of their eyes is a shade of dark brown. The eye rims of the Bouvier des Flandres are black not lacking of pigment. The haw of it is hardly visible.

The ears of the bouvier are situated high and alert. Should the ears be cropped, the ears are to be a triangular shape and should be in proper measurement to the size of the cranium. The inner corners of the ears of the bouvier have to be in line with the outer corner of the canine's eyes. Should the bouviers ears be situated too low or too closely set together are seen as serious faults.

The skull of the bouvier is to be well developed as it is flat. The head should be slightly less wide than long. When seen from the side, the utmost lines of the dog's skull along with its muzzle must be parallel. The skull of the bouvier should be seen wide between the ears, and the frontal groove should be barely marked.

The stop is a lot more apparent than it is real, because of the upstanding eyebrows. The measurements of the length of the skull to the length of the muzzle is 3 is to 2. The muzzle of the bouvier is broad, powerful, well filled and defined. The muzzle tapers gradually leading toward the nose of the dog without it ever showing to be pointed. If a muzzle is shown to be narrow it is to be faulted.

The nose of the bouvier is large, and is black in colour. The nose is to be well developed as it is round at the edges and flared nostrils. Serious fault is found when a bouvier's nose is shown as a brown, pink or spotted colour. The cheeks of the bouvier are lean and flat with the dog's lips shown to be dry and tight fitting.

The jaws of the bouvier are powerful and are shown to be equal in length. The Bouvier des Flandres teeth are powerful, healthy and white in colour, with the canine's incisors meeting in a scissors bite. Teeth that are seen to be overshot or undershot are to be strongly penalized.

Neck, Topline, and Body

The neck of the powerful Bouvier des Flandres is to be shown strong and muscular, with it widening gradually into the canine's shoulders. When the neck of the bouvier is viewed from the side, the neck is to be seen gracefully arched with a proud carriage. When the neck of the bouvier is shown to be short or squatty, it is to be faulted. There should be no dewlap. The back of the neck is to be seen short, broad, and well-muscled having a firm level with the topline. The neck is to be seen and feel as supple and flexible bearing no signs of weakness.

The body or the trunk of the bouvier is to be seen and felt as powerful, wide and short. The chest of the bouvier is to be broad, with the brisket enlarging to the elbow of the bouvier in depth. The ribs of this canine are deep and visibly well sprung. The first ribs of the bouvier are somewhat bent. The other ribs are to be well sprung and absolutely well sloped as it nears the rear, giving the body the correct depth to the chest of the bouvier. To be strongly penalized is flat ribs or slab sidedness.

The flanks and loins of the bouvier is to be seen short, as it is wide and well-muscled, with no signs of weakness. The abdomen are of the bouvier is to be slightly tucked up. The horizontal line of the back of the bouvier has to be cast unnoticeably back into the curvature of the dog's rump, which is characteristically wide.

If the dog's croup is seen sunken or slanted croup this is a serious fault. The tail of the bouvier is to be docked, with a remaining 2 or 3 vertebrae.

The tail of the bouvier should be set high and must be aligned normally with the canine's spinal column. The tail must be carried upright preferably when in motion. Should any dogs be born tailless it should not be penalized for this missing appendage.

Forequarters

The forequarters of the Bouvier des Flandres should be strong boned, as it is well muscled and straight. The shoulders of the bouvier are comparatively long; it must be muscular but should not be loaded, appearing with a good layback. The shoulder blades of the bouvier as well as its humerus are roughly the same in length. It should form an angle a bit greater than 90 degrees when the dog is standing. A dog with steep shoulders is to be faulted. Elbows that are too close to the body and are parallel; if the elbows reach too far out or too far in, these are to be considered as faults. The forearms of the bouvier when viewed from either profile or when viewed from the front must be perfectly straight.

It should be parallel to one another and has to be perpendicular to the ground. They should be well muscled as it is strong boned. The carpus must be exactly in line with the forearms of the dog. It must be strong boned. Pasterns are to be short and slightly sloped. Dewclaws can be eliminated. Both its forefeet as well as hind feet should be rounded as they are compact. They should not turn in nor should they turn out; the toes are to be close and perfectly arched. It should have strong black nails and thick tough pads.

Hindquarters

The hindquarters of the Bouvier des Flandres are to be firm, adequately muscled with big, strong hams. The hindquarters of the bouvier should be in line with the dog's front legs when seen from either front or back. The legs are to be moderately long, should be well muscled. They should neither be too straight or too inclined. The thighs of the dog are to be wide and muscular.

The higher thigh of the dog must neither be too straight, nor should they slope too much. There should be moderate angulation at the stifle. The hocks of the bouvier are to be strong, and rather close to the ground. When it is standing and when seen from the back, the thighs should be unswerving and perfectly aligned with each other. When the Bouvier des Flandres is in motion, its forequarters must not turn in, nor should they turn out.

There should be a moderate angulation at the hock joint. Sickle or cow-hocks are found to be serious faults. The metatarsal bones in the hocks and feet are to be hardy and lean, should be rather cylindrical and perpendicular to the ground when the dog is standing. Should the dog be born with dewclaws, these are to be eliminated. Both forelegs and hindquarters should have the same measure and orientation.

Coat

The coat of the bouvier des flandres is to be tousled without being curly. The fur on the skull of the bouvier is to be short. On the upper part of the back of the bouvier, the coat should be particularly close and harsh constantly whilst remaining rough.

A bouviers fur is shaggy, disheveled and is a double coat that is able to withstand the most difficult work in the coldest of weather. The bouviers outer hairs are harsh and rough with a fine undercoat that is supple and thick. The coat of the bouvier des flandres may be trimmed a little only to accentuate the dog's body line. Over trimming that change the dog's naturally rugged look is to be avoided at all costs. The topcoat of the bouvier should be dry, harsh and trimmed to the touch and should have a length of about 2½ inches. A bouvier with a coat that is too long or too short is to be faulted and so with a coat that is too silky or woolly.

The mustache and beard of the bouvier is to be very dense, with the fur showing stubby and rugged on the higher side of the muzzle. The upper lip of the bouvier showing a thick mustache the chin heavy and rough with its beard permits the gruff expression that is characteristic of the bouvier des flandres breed. Its eyebrows and the erect hairs accentuate the form of the eyes without covering either of them.

The ears are to be rough - coated and the undercoat of the ears should have a thick mass of fine, closely cropped hair that is denser during the winter. As with the topcoat, the coat of the bouvier should form a water-resistant cover. When the dog has a flat coat, this means there is a lack of undercoat and should be considered a serious fault.

Color

The coat colours of the bouvier ranges from fawn to black, going through salt and pepper, then to gray and brindle. When apparent in a bouvier, a tiny white star on the chest is allowed. There is no one color to be favored other than that which is chocolate brown, parti-color, or white, which are to be severely penalized.

Gait

The entire being of the Bouvier des Flandres has to be balanced and well-proportioned to give it a free, strong and proud manner of walking. The extension of the front legs has to compensate for and must be in balance with the driving force of the back legs. The back legs, as it moves in a trot, shall stay firm and flat. Generally, the bouvier's gait is to be the logical proof of the construction and assembly of the dog. It is to be observed that while it moves at a quick trot, the well assembled Bouvier will have a tendency to single-track.

Temperament

The Bouvier des flandres is an even-tempered dog, steadfast, purposeful and courageous. A brutal or meek dog is not desirable.

Famous Bouvier des Flandres

The Belgian Cattle Dog, better known as the bouvier des flandres has been a well-loved dog by many people from the time they emerged on the farms of Belgium. It is a commanding, strong, powerful dog that is smart, independent and quick to learn what it is taught.

Bouviers also have a deep need and desire to have a close relationship with a human. They are deserving of a home that treats them as members of the family. They need to be involved and immersed in your daily family activities and need to be utilized the way they are meant to. Although best suited for families living on a farm or in houses with big yards and free rolling land, a bouvier may live comfortably in an apartment or condominium as long as its owners understand that the bouviers will need to be let out and let loose often. Not doing so will make the bouvier develop a nasty temper, will make it become ill-mannered and overall, not a very happy camper.

It is from the flancers area and used as a work dog on the farm, from herding cattle, protecting livestock and securing the safety of the family. They are not easily intimidated. They were used quite a bit during the two world wars and it was largely due to the dangerous work it was employed that the numbers of the bouvier dwindled in the past and was almost nonexistence. Thankfully, with the help and the passion of some dog lovers the, the numbers of the bouvier increased once again.

The breed has made a comeback in the past 70 years and has played an important role. Breeders now play an important role in preserving the genetics and the history of the dog. Bouviers in Europe are not docked or cropped like those found in the United States.

There have been several bouviers in the police service. They are thinkers and great intimidators. They are able to corral perpetrators as well as animals that go astray. They are very smart and utterly trainable especially when they are little. The challenge is if you are not consistent and you do not do the job properly, they will carry out what they seem as necessary. They are hardly to be categorized as a push button dog because they are able to figure out what they deem right.

They are hardworking dogs who are bred to work hard and work long hours on the range. They are a large-breed dog who enjoys about 10 - 12 years. They are great condominium dwellers. A good home for a bouvier is not the actual structure but the mental commitment owners give the bouvier the mental stimulation they need.

Go and look for work that allows the bouvier to utilize its great gifts of scouting, hunting, corralling, herding, sniffing, detecting and securing. Owning a bouvier can be challenging for a first time owner which is why it is vital that an owner knows how to be consistent with a bouvier and can lead the bouvier.

The training and socialization period is important and it is critical for an owner to understand this if they expect to have a bouvier who listens to and follows their commands.

Some of the more famous bouviers were owned by some of the most recognizable people in human history. The former president of the United States of America, Ronald Reagan owned a bouvier which he named Lucky. Lucky was gifted to the Reagan family in 1985. The dog was named after the mother of Nancy Reagan and was the more memorable of the two dogs the once First Couple of the White House owned. Lucky left a really great impression even though it moved out of the White House a little time after and spent the rest of its day on the Reagan farm.

Both Ronald and Nancy Reagan were dog lovers and were happy to take in Lucky, who almost always stole the show, as she dragged either Nancy or Ronald in directions they were not going. Lucky was a big dog who was almost feet tall and who weighed a hefty 80 pounds. Needless to say, and with pictures and video as proof, both the president and his first lady were practically dragged around by the poorly-trained bouvier.

When the 1999 film "A Dog from Flandres" came out there was much concern about the possible over-breeding and ill-breeding methods that were to later happen after the film showed. This was after the film feature of 101 Dalmatians and Beethoven came out. After the showing of the two films mentioned, the clamor for Dalmatians and St. Bernard breeds became so plentiful that the dogs which resulted from quick thoughtless breeding methods came out ill or lived a life full of medical issues. The over-breeding using malpractices caused very grave health problems.

This was the concern most dog lovers, especially bouvier breeders had after the showing of the film "A Dog from Flandres." Diane Keaton and Goldie Hawn was said to have been owners of bouvier des flandres as well. Bouvier dogs are excellent animals that are easy to train if given the proper teacher who is a proper leader and who is consistent, they can learn well and fast. The Bouvier des flandres are not for everyone. Since it is a highly intelligent dog it would need someone who commands greater respect and a steadfast commitment to the dog, especially during the training period because the bouvier can get pretty stubborn.

They have a very strong work ethic and will get jobs done smartly. Depending on where it is located, a bouvier des flandres is called by many different names; some call it the Vullibard or the dirty bearded dog, others (like those in France) call it Toucheur de boeuf or the Cattle Driver and then there are those who prefer to call it the Koehond or the Cow Dog.

Many owners of the bouvier say that the dog from Belgium is perhaps one of the sloppiest dogs they have seen because the beards and mustaches of the bouvier collects so much food debris, but more so, water. Their beards would collect up so much water that it would splash around even after they have taken a drink.

The rough estimate of the annual cost to own and maintain a bouvier is around US$600 to US$1000 - and this is just for food alone. On top of that, grooming and bathing costs can reach up to another $1000 per year on top of the food costs. That is a whopping $2000 in food and grooming alone! Adding to the cost mentioned would be collars, crates, bed, treats, feeding dishes, brushes, trimmers, and of course, vet bills.

A lot of bouvier owners have said that their bouviers thrive better with holistic and natural foods. It is even said that holistic feeding helps eliminate some health conditions which existed prior to feeding the bouvier natural food. The bouvier des flandres is said to rank as the most lovable as well as the greatest dogs by each and every owner who has owned a bouvier. The bouvier is an active dog, but will not take to exercise on its own. It will need to encouragement, support and prodding of its human to be able to teach them how much they love and need exercise.

Chapter Ten: Reminders and Summary

We have finally come to the end of the short compilation of things you need to know about the great Bouvier Des Flanders. We hope you have found this book a helpful guide as you get to know more about the Bouvier des Flandres and what it would take to raise one in your home. Here is a roundup of the things you need to keep in mind and things you should expect once you bring home your bouvier. The initial thing every Bouvier des flandres owner has to know is that the bouvier is in fact a breed that is distinct on its own.

The bouvier is a powerful, strong, robust, and loyal and one of the hardest working dogs around. It may be mistaken for one of the other big working dogs, but it is a breed on its own with its own strengths. The bouvier des flandres is canine who has the combination of the best traits of each and every breed - but it also has the same combination of the bad traits of all the dogs in the spectrum too.

The thing about owning a bouvier is that once you take it home, all the bad traits are stifled and overpowered by the sheer weight of its loyalty as well as the love it gives to the family who takes it in. The bouvier is a magnificent shaggy beast that is incomparable in character because the bouvier is one of the most loyal canine's you will come across. It is fearless and resolute. It is staunch and steadfast in its love and allegiance to you.

The bouvier des flanders is an unusual dog and can be quite an intimidating fellow towering above most other dogs. However, the bouvier draws just as much curiosity and beckons others to it because of it is not quite usual look and hairy features. This gentle giant is one that reserves its right to speak and is a fiercely protective dog that would throw itself at a suspected threat, instead of biting a person of ill-intention.

The bouvier can be a playful, mischievous and coy troublemaker who at the same time can show its friendly side, and would try to fit itself into your lap. It is a robust and playful dog who can sometimes throw its weight around so make sure that you supervise all play with tiny humans and tinier pets. It is a big teddy bear who just wants you to play with it, talk to it and who loves being around its humans. Continuous and rigid early training that should ideally begin at its 8th week of life will turn your little roughian of a teddy bear into one of the finest dogs around. It will be a delightful addition to your family who will endear itself to each family member and especially latch itself to one person in the family.

A bouvier des flandres is loyalty, companionship, warm love and more all rolled into one dog. The bouvier des flanders when young, can be quite a handful with its hairy and commanding physique. But it can be delivered out of the naughty, stubborn and mischievous puppyhood ways through intensive, yet kind, early puppy training. It can turn out to be the epitome of a well-mannered, well-behaved canine should its mistress or master gives it the proper time coupled with the proper amount of patience during training.

- The bouvier des flandres is a canine that measures at least 2 feet in height, from the withers, so you can imagine that it is quite a big dog. It may not be as big as other giant breed canines, but you may want to check your inherent spaces to see if you will be able to house a growing Bouvier Des Flanders. It is a shaggy-haired dog who will need constant maintenance every day and get its thick, dense coat groomed or it will run the risk of looking like a matted yak.

- The gentle-giant of a dog, with the proper training and socialization can turn into one of the most endearing dogs around who would come at you with a warm tongue and great big hugs. You will surely be making a lot of good memories with a properly trained and housebroken bouvier des flandres, but it will take a lot of work from your end to help it achieve that.

- The great, big, hairy bouvier is a loyal and loving canine who will be there to protect you and secure fort. It is a canine that is comfortable to live with and share house with. The bouvier for all its intelligence and independence can be drawn out of its stubborn streak. Take the time to for the most immediate and critical training it will get once it joins your ranks - potty training. Upon its arrival to your home, you want to impart this immediate and most important learning because it will be a critical training that will seal the bond between you and canine.

- The sooner that bouvier learn this, the more comfortable it will be to live with your bouvier. The affection and bond will grow as long as the new human it joins extends it enough patience and love during training. The easier a bouvier is to live with the more it is loved and revered by its human family.

- When potty training your new bouvier, make sure to spend an extra ten to fifteen minutes outdoors and allow your bouvier to relieve itself, not once but twice. The extra few minutes outdoors after the first "unloading" will serve you well since a young bouvier can get distracted and not be able to "get it all out" in one go. So take the extra few minutes outside lest you are ready to live with the bouvier taking a second "go" on your new carpet. The few extra minutes outside will pay off in the long run since the smart bouvier will begin to understand that outside time is also "nature" time.

- The bouvier if not given the proper socialization can be a handful. Socialization goes hand in hand with formal puppy training and it can be as simple as going to the park, the store or anywhere where it can be around other humans and pets. The time it gets to experience new things outside of your four walls will be an integral part of your young bouvier des flandres socialization. It needs to experience other things and learn to decide for itself what is acceptable and not. It needs to experience other people for itself to understand who is to stand close to you or if it needs to protect you. A bouvier will throw itself at something rather that stands it down with its barking.

- An ill-mannered bouvier can be an intimidating canine when faced with visitor and strangers it does not know. Little do these people know how much of a charmer it is. Whilst a bouvier with perfect manners can display unfaltering friendliness as well as its fearless nature, the bouvier is sensitive and can feel the verbal tones and body language of a person before it. This allows the bouvier to act according to the situation. It is in the bouviers nature to be trusting until it finds reason to suspect otherwise. Instinct is what signals the bouvier to protect its family. The mere presence of the bouvier will give any family or family member the measure of comfort and protection.

The bouvier des flandres likes to have fun just like you. It does enjoy dressing up so you can be sure to get your bouvier in the game during dress-up-season times. Halloween and Christmas is a great time to allow your bouvier to meet the neighborhood. Don on the bouvier dud of Halloween and make it your partner as you distribute candies and treats to little trick or treaters. Dress it up as a reindeer to haul a cart of gifts or a sled full of kids during the Christmas season and see the kids eyes light up with glee. It is a clown and loves to be part of a good and bigger cause. Bouviers can be great swimmers if taught early on with the proper swimming and diving training.

They are not the best hunters but they are great trackers. They play well and will gladly retrieve a ball for you until you get bored. Put them on high grade premium dog food so that they are odorless. But a good bath and a regimen of maintenance is needed to keep the bouvier clean and well-groomed.

Make sure that your bouvier is able to understand and follow commands because they will need to be given directions most especially when they step outside of your home. Do not allow your bouvier to be road accident victims because they are not able to take directives like "sit", "down", "come", "stay". Obedience commands will be very important for bouviers to understand and follow once they are ready to go out into the world with you.

Be mindful of medical conditions your bouvier can develop and learn to recognize when your bouvier is out of sorts and feeling uncomfortable. Most dogs over the age of 6 are can be and are prone to bloat. It is still undetermined how bloat in a dog comes about, but there has been suspicion that fast eating is one of the culprits. Avoid bloat and use slow feeding bowls when feeding your dog. The device is designed so that a dog does not wolf down its food too fast, allowing it to enjoy each bite and morsel in leisure thereby allowing it down its food in a slow manner giving it the proper time to digest its food.

Make certain that you get to know your dog to be able to tell when your dog in in discomfort. When your dog seems restless, when it seems like its wants to vomit but does not come up with anything, when it keeps moving around in a spot trying to get comfortable but with little to no result, when the dog whines, or when it snaps at it flanks or displays a distended stomach, your dog is likely to be suffering from bloat. It is not a common occurrence but it is something that can happen to all dogs therefore every dog owner should be aware of this too. This is so that you can avoid this from happening and for you to be able to identify when the dog has developed bloat. Should this happen, you want to bring your bouvier to the vet immediately.

Most working dogs develop hip dysplasia. Almost all dog lines have a tendency to develop it and it is yet unclear whether it is a genetically passed on condition or if it is one that develops in most active dogs. Whether it be one or the other (or both!), be aware that hip dysplasia can affect most dogs. Should you be looking into breeding your bouvier keep in mind that you will want to be part of the few who painstakingly work at improving the breed.

A pair of parent-dogs who have been certified free from hip dysplasia can produce hip dysplasia in their offspring. On the other hand a pair of parents who have mild forms of hip dysplasia could produce offspring that are clear of the condition. There are some tests available now that can give you a heads up on the possibility of the condition later, but it is not a guarantee because a mild condition can take up to 20 years to manifest itself in the dog and acutely affect the animal.

Bouviers are not heavy shredders. The coat of the bouvier will eventually blow out in chunks and the typical shedding in most dogs is not apparent in the bouvier. Make it a point to maintain the coat grooming of the bouvier des flandres regularly. The ideal coat appearance of a bouvier is a coat that is about 2 1/2 inches with an outcoat that is harsh and rough to the touch. The second layer or the underlying coat of the bouvier is dense, fine and soft. Unless you intend to show your bouvier, you can keep him untouched save for a good trim during spring along with general maintenance of ears, beard and head.

Bouviers are loyal as they are territorial as they are bonders. They are all these to their human wards and the fort they hold down. They will flank, shadow and follow you and their favourite family member around the house and go from room to room with you. It will stay by your side and accompany you on walks errands and jobs you need to do around the house or your lot. It will help you as long as you remember to give it chores.

It is not unusual to hear about bouvier des flandres who never venture out of their bounds, but make sure that you have a leash (and that it is trained to be on one) for times when you have to take out your dog where there is traffic or other dogs. You don't want to run the risk of your investigative dog running out into the street where there is oncoming traffic. They can also leap over a fence that is five feet high, if they have reason to, but they will normally prefer to keep guard and stock of home.

Bouviers will bark out and call for you when they do not see you just to know if you are within reach and are near, most especially pups, and this is why crate training is important to the pup. Crate training must not feel like punishment instead crate training should allow your dog to understand boundaries and it also gives the canine a measure of comfort.

Crate training allows the canine to learn about potty training as well. If you are an individual who needs to be out of the house for extended periods of time, place your young bouvier des flandres in a crate whilst you are away. You will soon see that the pups understand their crate to be their den which gives them security and protection.

You want to start training your bouvier puppy to get used to being in its crate/den by putting the dog in its crate. You want to move as far away from the crate and go to where you can't hear or see him and where he can't see or hear you either. Your bouvier des flandres will soon learn that the crate is meant to give him some peace and quiet.

All dogs as a rule, bark, jump and chew and so goes the same for bouviers IF not given the proper early training. Make sure that you start training your smart bouvier early and allow it to learn how to tell wrong from right. Depending on its age, chewing is in fact a reality for most young, teething bouviers, so make sure to put out the correct kind of chew toys, sticks and bones where the dog has access. Scatter these around the house and your yard so that your young bouvier has access to any one of them at any given time. If you do not do this you run the risk of your bouvier gnawing at a favourite sofa, chair or table and causing destruction around the house.

Here are a few more things to remember before you head out to get in touch with a breeder for your very own bouvier buddy:

- Make sure that you spend sufficient downtime with your new buddy regularly because like with every relationship on the build, you want to get to know the little quirks and characteristics that make your bouvier an individual. Getting to know your bouvier des flandres gives you a better edge and advantage as you take care of them. You also want to get the services of a vet who is well versed on taking care of the tough and highly tolerant bouvier.

- Make sure that you are financially capable, and ready to take on the responsibilities of raising a bouvier. Not only will it take a big chunk from your weekly and monthly bills but the needs of the bouvier will not come cheap at a whopping $2000 at its bare minimum annually. Make sure that you are in the financial position to take one in to raise. You don't want to be one of the people who later on realize they can't afford the responsibilities and challenges of raising a bouvier and later on giving up the bouvier in a shelter.

- Pay mind that the bouvier you take in gets the proper outside time for it to stretch out and do its business. But most of all, you as its new human, will need to stimulate and engage its mind the most. A bored bouvier is not a pretty picture. Make it a point that the bouviers mind is engaged positively so that it stays out of trouble and causes you very little.

- Choose to feed your bouvier the proper sort of food that would promote good skin, coat and health. The overall health of your bouvier hinges in the history of the parent of your puppy as well as the food you give it. Giving it the proper balanced nutrition will allow the bouvier to thrive at its best and grow to the smart intelligent, well-mannered dog it is meant to be. Make sure that you channel all that pent up energy in the proper areas of its canine life.

- Network with other bouvier des flandres owners from whom you can learn more about living with a bouvier. Take every advice with caution and remember that a solution for one does not necessarily mean a solution for all. You bouvier is an individual on its own who deserves the time to be known.

You will be sure to enjoy your bouvier if you put in the equal effort and time to train your new bouvier. As much as many say that bouvier aren't for first time dog owners, the most important thing to remember is the intensity of commitment a person is willing to give and extend to the dog. Dedication to the discipline and learning of your dog is important when taking in a dog and is doubly true for when you decide to raise a bouvier des flandres.

As much as it is a unique dog that comes with its own set of challenges, if you are a first time dog owner choosing to raise a bouvier, and if you put in the commitment to raising this dog along with an equal amount of consistency, applied with strong leadership, you will be able to successfully raise your bouvier with confidence.

We bid you many joyous days with your loyal and loving bouvier!

Glossary of Dog Terms

Achondroplasia: Abnormal development of cartilage found at the ends of the long bones; resulting to a congenital dwarfism.

Acquired Immunity: Immunity achieved through the injection of antiserum or development of antibodies.

Agility Trials: Competition organized at which dogs undergo a series of obstacles and jumps.

All-Breed Show: A type of conformation show where all AKC-recognized breeds are allowed to be exhibited.

Almond Eyes: Shape of the eyes that are elongated rather than rounded

American Kennel Club: It is an organization founded and established in line with the laws of the State of New York for purebred dogs events

Barrel Hocks: A.k.a spread hocks, a type of hocks that turn out

Barring: Markings that are stripes

Beady: Used to describe small, round, and glittering eyes.

Beard: The long hair growing and can be seen on the underjaw.

Collar: A material used to restrain a dog. Usually made from nylon, leather or chain. It is also where the leash is attached.

Colitis: A kind of inflammation in the colon.

Dermatitis: A kind of Inflammation in the skin.

Distemper: A viral disease of dogs that is very infectious often characterized by a catarrhal discharge from the eyes and nose, loss of appetite, vomiting, fever, and partial paralysis.

Dog Fancy: Used to denote a group of people who are actively interested in the promotion of purebred dogs.

Dog Show: Also called as conformation show, It is where dogs are judged on how closely they met their own breed standards

Enteritis: A kind of inflammation in the intestinal tract

Entropion: A genetic condition that is complexly resulting in the turning in of the eyelid; causes corneal ulceration.

Even Bite: Also known as the level bite, it means the meeting of upper and lower incisors exactly.

Fallow: Pale cream to light fawn color; pale yellow; yellow-red. Color definitions may vary by breed. Always check the breed standard for the definitive color description.

Feathering: It is the long fringe of hair found on the legs, ears, body, or tail.

Flying Ears: It is characterized by semi-prick ears and drop ears that can stand or fly

Gait: It is the walk in general or the pattern of footsteps at various rates of speed

Groom: Keeping the neatness of your dog by means of brushing, combing, or trimming

Groups: Includes the groups that the AKC has made; working, toy, sporting, hound, non-sporting, herding, and terrier

Hip Dysplasia: It is a condition wherein the hip joint is abnormally formed

Hormone: It is usually a peptide or steroid that may be responsible growth or metabolism.

Humane Societies: Groups advocating to fight and stop animal and human abuse

Hypothermia: A condition wherein the body is exposed to a very cold environment causing an abnormally low body temperature

Inbreeding: It is the mating of two dogs who are closely related and of the same breed.

Inflammation: It refers to the redness, pain, and swelling of the skin tissues caused by injury, irritation, or infection.

Injection: It refers to a dose of liquid medicine that is being injected into the body.

Iris: It is a colored membrane neighboring the pupil of the eye.

Jacobson's Organ: It is a sense organ found in the roof of the dog's mouth. The function of this organ is between smell and taste.

Jowls: It is the flesh of the jaws and lips

Kennel: An enclosed building where dogs are being kept.

Kennel Cough: Also known as Tracheobronchitis of dogs

Kink Tail: It is characterized by a deformity in the caudal vertebrae

Knuckling Over: It is a condition wherein the wrist joint is faulty structured allowing it to flex forward due to the standing dog's weight

Leather: It denotes the ear's flap or the outer ear buoyed by cartilage and surrounding tissue.

Leptospirosis: A kind of disease that is infectious to domestic animals.

Luxating Patella: Th condition wherein the kneecap slips when the joint is moved. This problem is transmitted genetically and can potentially lead to lameness

Luxation: Anatomical structure's dislocation

Maternal Immunity: A kind immunity that is temporary and can be passed from a mother to her offspring while inside the uterus

Microchip: A device as small as a grain of rice encoded with a unique number. This is implanted underneath the skin of your dog.

Molars: It is the posterior teeth of the dental arcade, with two on each side of the upper jaw and three on each side in the lower jaw in an adult with correct dentition.

Natural Breed: This refers when a breed of dog occurred naturally even without the need for selective breeding.

Neuter: The process of castrating or spaying.

Nick: A kind breeding that can produce desirable puppies.

Nictitating Membrane: It is the inner eyelids of some mammals, birds, and reptiles that are transparent. Also known as the third eyelid.

Obedience Trial: This is an event in line with the rules of AKC at which an obedience degree can be merited

Obesity: It is a condition characterized by an excessive accumulation of fat leading to the state of being overweight or obese.

Omnivore: A person or animal that eats both vegetable and animal substances

Ovulate: The process of producing ova or the discharging of eggs from the ovary

Parvovirus: A disease of canines that is highly contagious and fatal.

Pedigree: It is a record of a dog's genealogy of three generations or more which is usually written.

Phenotype: It is the observable biochemical or physical characteristics of an organism determined with the help of environmental influences and genetic makeup.

Quarantine: Enforced isolation or restriction of free movement imposed to prevent the spread of contagious disease.

Quick: It is the vein that runs through a dog's nails or claw

Registries: These are the organizations responsible for keeping the official records on specific subjects with respect to dogs.

Reward: It is something positive like treats or praise usually utilized as a motivating factor to stimulate desired behavior

Saddle: These are the markings in the shape of a saddle that can be found on the back.

Scent: It is the odor left by any animal in trail

Shock: A massive physiological reaction that is temporarily caused by severe emotional or physical trauma.

Show Quality: A dog pedigreed to meet the official breed standard, therefore, becoming fit to compete in dog shows.

Topical: A kind of drug applied on a localized surface of the body

Topline: The outline of the dog from behind the withers up to the tail

Trail: Hunting through smelling the scent of the ground

Undercoat: A soft and dense short coat covered by a longer top coat.

Underline: A combination of contours in connection with the brisket and the abdominal floor.

Utility Dog (UD): A dog rewarded by the AKC as a Utility Dog in line with his winnings towards certain minimum scores.

Vaccine: It is a preparation towards killed or weakened pathogen, usually a bacterium or virus

Walk: It is the gaiting pattern wherein three legs are supporting the body at all times on which feet are lifting on the ground in a regular sequence

Wind: Catching the scent of game.

Winging: A fault in the gaiting on which one or both front feet twist outward while the limbs are swinging forward.

Xiphoid Process: The sternum's cartilage process

Zoonosis: Used to denote certain disease of animals that can be easily transmitted to humans like rabies or psittacosis

Zygomatic Arch: It is a ridge that is bony extending posteriorly from under the eye orbit.

Photo Credits

Photo by user Jan Rifkinson via Flickr.com,
https://www.flickr.com/photos/janrif/2284893454/

Photo by user raddewey via Flickr.com,
https://www.flickr.com/photos/raddewey/2428732132/

Photo by user Jan Rifkinson via Flickr.com,
https://www.flickr.com/photos/janrif/2280475672/in/photostr
eam/

Photo by user rmcnicholas via Flickr.com,
https://www.flickr.com/photos/rmcnicholas/4673201536/

Photo by user Jan Rifkinson via Flickr.com,
https://www.flickr.com/photos/janrif/2340220511/in/photostr
eam/

Photo by user Jan Rifkinson via Flickr.com,
https://www.flickr.com/photos/janrif/2280475398/in/photostr
eam/

Photo by user Jan Rifkinson via Flickr.com,
https://www.flickr.com/photos/janrif/2280331200/

Photo by user Renée Hubregtse – Koks via Flickr.com,
https://www.flickr.com/photos/superneej/3119188048/

Photo by user Svenska Mässan via Flickr.com,
https://www.flickr.com/photos/svenskamassan/23683385663/

Photo by user Pierre-Jean Vidal via Flickr.com,
https://www.flickr.com/photos/131306161@N08/17070650620
/

References

"Aortic/Subaortic Stenosis" – Cornell.edu
http://vet.cornell.edu/hospital/Services/Companion/Cardiolo
gy/conditions/subaortic-stenosis.cfm

"Bouvier des flandres" – AKC.org
http://www.akc.org/dog-breeds/bouvier-des-flandres/

"Bouvier des flandres" – Petmd.com
http://www.petmd.com/dog/breeds/c_dg_bouvier_des_fland
res

"Bouvier des flandres" – HomesteadOntheRange.com
https://homesteadontherange.com/2017/05/24/bouvier-des-
flandres/

"Bouvier Des Flandres Dog Breed Information and
Personality Traits" – The Hillspet
https://www.hillspet.com/dog-care/dog-breeds/bouvier-des-
flandres

"Bouvier des flandres Care" – AKC.org
http://www.akc.org/dog-breeds/bouvier-des-flandres/care/

"Bouvier des Flandres Health Care & Feeding" -
YourPureBredPuppy.com
http://www.yourpurebredpuppy.com/health/bouvierdesflan
dres.html

"Glaucoma in Dogs" – Petmd.com
http://www.petmd.com/dog/conditions/eyes/c_dg_glaucom
a

"How to Take Care of Your Bouvier des Flandres" –
AnimalCareTip.com
http://animalcaretip.com/how-to-take-care-of-your-bouvier-
des-flandres/

"The Dog That Got in "Der Fueher's Face" - DieselPunks.org
http://www.dieselpunks.org/profiles/blogs/that-which-got-
in-der-fueher-s-face

"The Hitler Vendetta Myth" - AngelPlace.net
http://www.angelplace.net/Angel/HitlerVendettaMyth.htm

Feeding Baby
Cynthia Cherry
978-1941070000

Axolotl
Lolly Brown
978-0989658430

Dysautonomia, POTS
Syndrome
Frederick Earlstein
978-0989658485

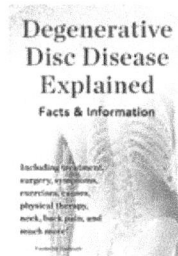

Degenerative Disc
Disease Explained
Frederick Earlstein
978-0989658485

Sinusitis, Hay Fever,
Allergic Rhinitis Explained
Frederick Earlstein
978-1941070024

Wicca
Riley Star
978-1941070130

Zombie Apocalypse
Rex Cutty
978-1941070154

Capybara
Lolly Brown
978-1941070062

Eels As Pets
Lolly Brown
978-1941070167

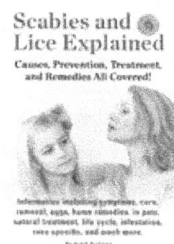

Scabies and Lice Explained
Frederick Earlstein
978-1941070017

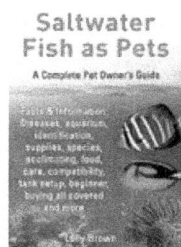

Saltwater Fish As Pets
Lolly Brown
978-0989658461

Torticollis Explained
Frederick Earlstein
978-1941070055

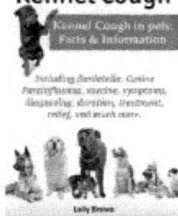

Kennel Cough
Lolly Brown
978-0989658409

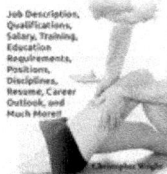

Physiotherapist, Physical
Therapist
Christopher Wright
978-0989658492

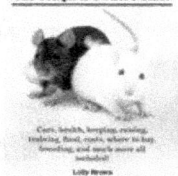

Rats, Mice, and Dormice
As Pets
Lolly Brown
978-1941070079

Wallaby and Wallaroo Care
Lolly Brown
978-1941070031

Bodybuilding Supplements
Explained
Jon Shelton
978-1941070239

Demonology
Riley Star
978-19401070314

Pigeon Racing
Lolly Brown
978-1941070307

Dwarf Hamster
Lolly Brown
978-1941070390

Cryptozoology
Rex Cutty
978-1941070406

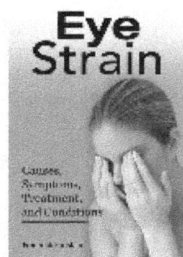

Eye Strain
Frederick Earlstein
978-1941070369

Inez The Miniature Elephant
Asher Ray
978-1941070353

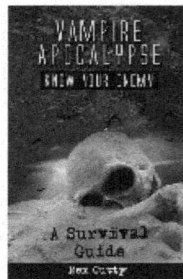

Vampire Apocalypse
Rex Cutty
978-1941070321

www.ingramcontent.com/pod-product-compliance
Lightning Source LLC
Chambersburg PA
CBHW052126090426
42741CB00009B/1968